FINDING MY OWN LION

BRIAN ALBA

This book was created with the purpose of being calm in difficult times, mainly conditioned on ways in which one can get ahead and succeed in life despite adversities or limitations.

It is designed to motivate and to find the encouragement that is often lacking, especially in the times we are currently living in.

This book is not offering individualized advice or advice tailored to a particular type of person or to treat any specific disease or condition of anyone. If you have any type of illness, condition or particular need, please seek the services of a professional.

The author specifically disclaims any responsibility for any discomfort or risk of any kind incurred as a direct or indirect consequence of the use and application of any of the contents of this book.

I would like to dedicate this book to all those people who have gone through difficult moments in life and have found the strength to keep going. To those who have lost hope at some point and have found their way back to the light. To all the brave ones who have decided to take control of their lives and have created their own path towards success and happiness.

With love and gratitude.

TABLE OF CONTENTS

PROLOGUE

Personal development is a very broad term that perhaps many know and will say more of the same! But it is really important to read and study on this topic. Many think that they can help themselves alone, and that is not true; it is always necessary to have a guide and study the subject to move forward and get rid of many things that can stagnate us and not allow us to be truly happy.

And what is happiness? In this book, we will see a little about that, how the world has changed, and how sometimes we get stuck in our past, not allowing us to move forward and achieve full happiness; I tell you that I grew up in the midst of negative beliefs that did not let me grow. as a person, here I tell you a little about this experience.

We will also see how the concept of happiness has been distorted, thinking that it is only about material goods, but if you are not happy inside, nothing that comes from the outside can give you that happiness.

In short, money does not guarantee happiness; it is guaranteed by what is in your mind and heart. But we must seek prosperity and get ahead; just draw your plan, free yourself from the past and do it... because ultimately, you can be the king of the world.

CHAPTER 1

THE WORLD HAS CHANGED

ORIGINS

December 2019

December is a very significant month for most people around the world; for the Catholic Christian religion, to cite an example, it is a month of great importance since they celebrate the birth of Jesus. Despite regardless of religion, nationality, race or social class, December will always be a month full of hope for everyone since it ends a year that was endowed with experiences, experiences and/ or learning and the expectation of a better future in the year that is about to begin, this is an undoubted reality in most of the cultures of humanity.

By the time December 2019 arrived, the world continued its course as normal; humanity continued with its daily chores, planning and arranging for tomorrow as if it were in our hands; I write this in the sense that some people We tend to believe that tomorrow is ours, and we can decide what will be of our life, I do not write it in the sense of planning. Planning is good, necessary and healthy; believing that we have absolute control and obsess over tomorrow is not convenient.

In short, in December 2019, each one of us found ourselves locked up where we usually live, our own reality; a news was heard worldwide to which some people gave importance, but many others did not give it anything of importance since they did not know It was about an event that involved them, or so they thought, they forgot the fact that we are all connected whether we like it or not, this is our true essence, we cannot detach ourselves from the challenge of humanity, be it the nation, whatever it is from another continent, are the majority of the people from that place from another religion, from another language. The truth is that we are united in this world, and what happens somewhere, either directly or indirectly, influences everything.

In Wuhan (China) an infectious disease caused by the outbreak of the Coronavirus pathogen, the most recently discovered to date, had broken out, and we were hearing news about COVID-19. SARS-CoV-2 (severe acute respiratory syndrome coronavirus type 2), the virus was first identified by the hospital admission of a group of sick people with an unknown type of pneumonia; most of the first admissions were related to workers from south china Wuhan seafood wholesale market.

The virus behaved in an expansive-aggressive manner, and China saw the need to come out quickly in defense of its inhabitants, with the construction of isolation hospital centers in a few days for those infected, the way and the short time in which China managed to build its hospital centers, caused greater surprise and admiration in the rest of the nations of the world, than the alarm of the virus that was about to spread. However, there was no shortage of those who asked themselves questions such as: if this virus reaches my country, can our government assume the ravages of this pathogen?; Do we have the capacity to organize ourselves as they have organized in China?

Sooner rather than later, the month of March arrived, and Covid19 had already spread to almost all countries in the world. On March 11, 2020, the World Health Organization (WHO) ruled naming the Covid-19 pandemic a pandemic! Just over a century after the last pandemic to the world, the 1918 influenza known as the "Spanish Flu," which killed 1/3 of the world's population; A pandemic arrived with a pathogen that baffled us all because we knew nothing about it: it changed life directly or indirectly for all of humanity. The WHO announced the following:

“The virus is generally transmitted from person to person through small droplets of saliva, known as Flügge droplets, which are emitted when speaking, sneezing, coughing or breathing. It is spread mainly when people are in close contact, but it can also be spread by touching a contaminated surface and then bringing contaminated hands to the face or mucosa.”

Recommended prevention measures include handwashing, covering your cough, a physical distancing between people, and wearing masks, as well as self-isolation and monitoring for people suspected of being infected."

With the declared pandemic and the prevention recommendations of the WHO, given the growing number of positive cases of Covid-19 and its high mortality rate in the world, most countries have declared a state of total quarantine. School classes at the initiation, primary, secondary and university levels were suspended until further notice; any public recreational activity such as cinemas, parks, and any entertainment centers were closed until further notice; work activities were also suspended except for those of the life-saving sectors such as health, the military, fire brigades, civil defense and the food industry. All this was done in order to protect humanity from such a devastating pandemic.

However, even with the declaration of quarantine in most of countries of the world, the cases of Covid-19 continued to grow, and each country bore the responsibility of solving the consequences that were generated by the pandemic. Many people ignored the existence of the virus, and instead of social distancing, which is why the quarantine was declared, they took the opportunity to meet at parties and clandestine activities with medium and large groups of people, which further generated the expansion of the virus. Virus; another notable consequence was the reduction of staff in many workplaces since the companies were not generating income and could not maintain so many employees.

Beyond all this, this virus has left us with many other collateral damages that we have not yet finished radicalizing and that, on the contrary, has taken on a new flavor of which, although humanity is expected to be more aware, we do not know what to expect. Because if the first knowledge of Covid-19 made something very clear to us, it is that we cannot take it for granted that it will happen tomorrow.

THE CONSEQUENCES

Distancing

It is no secret to anyone that a human being is a social being. Beyond our differences, all of us have the concept of society rooted in our DNA, for a reason God allowed us to come into the world in the bosom of a family.

Social distancing has had multiple consequences, both for people who did not abide by it, of which a large majority became seriously ill or sickened their families, and another large minority became ill without symptoms and spread the virus even more. I believe that when this virus becomes radicalized or when the vaccine is effective, and all countries have access to it, in a few years, they will begin to tell emotional personal stories, as happened with the Titanic story; there will be countless stories of people who lost to one of his grandparents, that old man who had not left home because he remembered the story that his parents told him about the Spanish flu pandemic and then, being aware and wanting to live, he complied with isolation, but his children came,

I think that from this experience, the families that went through this should have learned that:

"Love is not necessarily physical contact."

There will also be the talk of cases in which children became ill due to the undoubted mistake of declaring the virus only harmful to the elderly, parents who did not find how to entertain the infant sent him to play at the door of his house with The neighbor's children, a neighbor who has a brother who could not distance himself because he had to work selling anything as a town crier because if the virus did not kill him, hunger would kill him, so without any symptoms, his relatives were sick, among them his nephew who infected his neighborhood friends and as every basic statistics student knows the probability of an event occurring is 50%, one or more of these children did present symptoms, worsened and could or could not have died, but the point is that they should never have gotten sick.

I think that from this experience, the families that went through this should have learned not to trust what they do not know and not to underestimate a virus; our children are not a game, they are the most precious thing we have, and it is our primary duty to protect them.

Many stories will be told in relation to Covid-19; probably given how expansive the virus was and the large number of people it attacked, we will not learn many interesting anecdotes, but hopefully, everyone has personally learned something fundamental from this event. And can pass it on to the future generation.

Now, what was clear from the beginning regarding the virus was that distancing and biosecurity measures were the only way to keep you safe; it spread rapidly through different media, including social networks in all countries of the world. Even in countries in which their government systems did not comply with the quarantine, campaigns of: "do not go out if it is not necessary and if necessary, do not go out without your face mask"; Stay at home! We will meet again! Among other slogans, the highest leader of the Catholic Church, Pope Francis, also made his voice heard by proclaiming, "Charity is prevention."

10 months after the declaration of the pandemic and the preventive measures taken, many sectors continued to be greatly affected, although many productive sectors were incorporated little by little in most countries and with all the biosecurity measures, let us remember that Starting the pandemic in many countries there were massive layoffs, leaving entire families not only at the expense of the virus but also unable to face COVID-19 and other diseases and situations.

How did COVID-19 and isolation affect children and adolescents?

In the education sector, a large part of the measures that countries have adopted in the face of the crisis caused by COVID-19 are related to the suspension of face-to-face classes at all levels. This situation has led to the deployment of distance learning modalities through the use of a diversity of formats and platforms, all this in order to prevent the spread of the virus and reduce its consequences.

However, great concern has been seen in the educational and family environment because, although professionals in the area of education, educational institutions and students, in general, have tried to adapt to the new situation, there is an undoubted truth and that is that not all students can keep up with this modality.

Not all students learn in the same way, and not all student communities have the necessary resources to face a distance education. When I talk about resources, I am not only referring to the appropriate technology but also to the face-to-face support of a tutor at home, such as one of the parents who guides them in part of the activities; this is because many times, the parents are not fully qualified to explain their children school subjects.

The foregoing has caused difficulties of all kinds, children and young people who cannot do their evaluation activities because they do not understand a subject are distressed, and parents who cannot fully help their children in these activities are frustrated; this is without counting the few cases of children and adolescents who have not endured the pressure and have come to attempt against their lives.

Those same groups that so many times we asked the same young people not to live so much within them, and today we present them as the only alternative, even though we explain to our youth that confinement is for their own good, no matter how intelligent they are and they understand how the virus develops, no matter how much philosophy we talk about that it is better to take shelter now to be able to live tomorrow, they are not going to accept it, they will obviously obey, but internally they will be in a fight with themselves because it is a complicated situation for them. A social being. Add to this the stress of parents who have lost their jobs due to downsizing and not being able to control their emotions of anger and distress; they are not very good with their children. No matter how much we explain to our youth that confinement is for their own good, no matter how intelligent they are and understand how the virus develops, no matter how much philosophy we talk to them regarding the fact that it is better to protect themselves now to be able to live tomorrow. They will not accept it, they will obviously obey, but internally they will be in a fight with themselves because it is a complicated situation for a social being. Add to this the stress of parents who have lost their jobs due to downsizing and not being able to control their emotions of anger and distress; they are not very good with their children. No matter how much we explain to our youth that confinement is for their own good, no matter how intelligent they are and understand how the virus develops, no matter how much philosophy we talk to them regarding the fact that it is better to protect themselves now to be able to live tomorrow, they will not accept it, they will obviously obey, but internally they will be in a fight with themselves because it is a complicated situation for a social being. Add to this the stress of parents who have lost their jobs due to downsizing and not being able to control their emotions of anger and distress; they are not very good with their children. They will not accept it; obviously, they will obey, but internally they will be in a fight with themselves because it is a complicated situation for a social being. Add to this the stress of parents who have lost their jobs due to downsizing and not being able to control their emotions of anger and distress; they are not very good with their children. They will not accept it; obviously, they will obey, but internally they will be in a fight with themselves because it is a complicated situation for a social being. Add to this the stress of parents who have lost their jobs due to downsizing and not being able to control their emotions of anger and distress; they are not very good with their children.

And then how were our emotions affected?

Although most people in the world had heard something about the news of the appearance of COVID-19 in Asia, specifically in China, very few people expected that this pathogen would not reach their continent, much less their country, city, community, family end to his life, but abruptly the day came for each nation in which the first cases of infection were determined and with them the uncertainty and concern of the majority and the spread of the virus, which affected men, women, children and adolescents regardless of creed, race or social status, if we could be sure of anything at first, it is that the behavior of the virus was not selective, and although at first it was classified as lethally dangerous only for elderly men and women, little by little it was determined that once again we were wrong with our habit of underestimating and cases of people of all ages who had been exposed to the virus and became seriously ill were appearing by country and by city.

Human beings are socially and colossally emotional, emotions are always present in each one, and influence our way of thinking and our way of acting in circumstances of great confusion, it is normal to experience intense changes in our emotions, the unexpected arrival of COVID -19 to our lives was a source of much confusion which caused dramatic changes in the emotions of some people, for example, they could very well be in a state of tranquility at home, probably happy because tomorrow they would not go to work and after hearing news about the arrival from the virus to the city in which he lives, he began to experience fear which minutes later turned into panic just at the moment he heard the neighbor sneezing, and remember that last week he was traveling to a nearby country and that place where his unfortunate neighbor visited for labor issues is being reported as the third country with the most positive cases of COVID-19, so it will be seen in less than 15 minutes he went from happy to anguished because of the pathogen that until then almost nobody knew anything about.

If we do not treat emotions in time, they intensify when we have excessive anguish or fear; it can become a real problem for us, affecting our interpersonal relationships due to having unfavorable attitudes neither for ourselves nor for others. It is for this reason that it is of great importance that we know ourselves and understand how we feel, as well as take charge of looking for practical and accessible strategies that help us control our emotions so as not to put our relationships with people around us at risk. In situations like the one we are still going through with COVID-19, it is essential to remember that it is also our duty to ensure that social isolation does not become distancing from the people we love.

The human brain is not designed to live in prolonged circumstances of uncertainty, and if COVID-19 brought an abundance of anything, it was exactly uncertainty at all levels, first of all, because it was an experience that humanity had not faced for a century. , then for having very little data on the virus, for not knowing if the measures taken by government entities were going to be appropriate and if our family was going to be able to support the measures taken financially, add to this the concern of children, adolescents and young university students who did not know how they were going to approach the new education system, the distance modality and which turned out to be somewhat fun, especially for those in the first years of primary and secondary education, but after spending more than two months at home and under the pressure of the activities they also began to present emotional problems, so the adults at home who did not even know how to help themselves with the collapse of emotions with which they were battling looked wrapped up in a new challenge, how I help my son who is suffering ravages from the pandemic.

How to manage to control emotions in times of pandemic?

The most important thing in the face of any crisis is not allowing negative emotions to control us. It is true that we still do not know for sure how everything related to COVID-19 will end, but it is also true that there is something that we can and must achieve to control are precisely our own emotions.

The main thing is to remain calm; only from serenity can we fight to overcome our negative emotions and get out of this life experience that, beyond the havoc, it leaves in each of us, is an experience.

To maintain peace of mind around oneself, it is of paramount importance to identify which situations are controllable by you and which situations are beyond your control, for example:

What can I control

*My attitude

*My respect for distancing

*My respect for Biosecurity measures

*Physical exercise at home

*Promotion of family activities

*What we do with time in terms of learning, and I enjoyed free moments with what they live by our side and with ourselves.

*The time we invest in social networks looking for information that, in most cases, could be speculation that generates calm and anguish.

What I can't control

*The time it will take for isolation or social distancing measures.

* The attitude of others.

*The respect of others for distancing and/or isolation

* The respect of others for Biosecurity measures.

We must then stop worrying about the things that we cannot control and take care of ourselves, focus our rational mind on those that we can, pay close attention to the reactions and actions that we have and redirect them positively, and create new routines that allow us to achieve achievements such as sessions of exercises at home will help us gain more confidence in ourselves and control our emotions more effectively, and influence our closest family.

I firmly believe that if this pandemic has helped us in any way, it is to be less confident in not taking things for granted; as has been said before, we must all plan; this is good, and this is healthy, but we must not obsess over tomorrow, since we are not there yet, all we have now is present, COVID-19 has caused not only loss of life for many of the people we know because although the virus has not touched either the person or the to your family if someone you know has been affected, more easily said, we all know someone who has lost one or more people due to COVID-19; however,

So somehow, most of us have undergone some change after the appearance of this devastating virus, which we have not yet radicalized, but everything indicates that we must learn to live with it even after most of humanity has the immunization system

How has COVID-19 affected the economy?

Most likely, the only thing that we can predict with certainty regarding the global crisis generated by COVID-19 is that it is not an issue to be resolved in the short term; it is predicted that it will probably take months or years before we return to a similar state to normal.

The repercussion of COVID-19 in Latin America will be significant due to the following:

+The decrease in exports

+Loss of principal

+The temporary succumbing of tourism

+ The temporary suspension of remittances

Although many Latin American countries are used to external shocks to their economic system, with the appearance of COVID-19 and the arrival of the pandemic, it is the first time that they have had to face so many challenges at once.

It is not a secret that for many Latin American countries, remittances are an important source of financing; if the economic difficulty is very deep and prolonged and/or causes unemployment in a developed country, it will be difficult for immigrants to sustain the flows that they send to their countries of origin. To date, everything seems to reveal that the US and Europe are going to be negatively affected by the COVID-19 pandemic, and these regions gather a large number of immigrants from Latin America. Among the affected countries, we have Mexico, Guatemala, the Dominican Republic, El Salvador, Honduras, Colombia and Venezuela, which was already particularly affected long before the appearance of COVID-19.

The confinement measures have directly impacted the economy of most Latin countries; this is due to the fact that in this region, approximately 50% of the population belongs to the informal sector and the mobility restrictions and closure of some businesses cause a noticeable impact on your income.

One of the political issues in the Latin American countries during the first period of the pandemic was related to the duration of the confinement and the opening of the economic sectors, some countries such as: Mexico and Brazil gave more esteem to sustaining economic activities than to The regulation of the pandemic, it has not yet been established whether this measure to keep national production active brought more costs than income with the spread of the virus throughout all its cities and sectors.

What most of the other countries tried to do was to support and support families and companies in order to keep them afloat; in this way, there could be production expenses once all the productive sectors gradually return to normal operation.

Another aspect to pay attention to is the fact that COVID-19, like other pathogens from previous pandemics, should decrease either by immunizing the population or by using medicines, which decreases its effects; for this reason, it has a lot of sense that the governments of the countries of

Latin America will create all possible fiscal spaces in the short term, with moderation, to guarantee macroeconomic sustainability after the pandemic, which is why during the course of the distancing measures, the governments allowed themselves to relax some rules with respect to the balance tax and debt.

The COVID-19 pandemic has produced a negative supply impact that has spread through demand restrictions; with this, it is evident that a global recession could originate, especially intense in European countries and the US. Latin America does not escape this reality. However, it has in its favor a series of advantages that would help it to recover more quickly than other parts of the world.

The population is relatively younger and the countries are less internationally connected, in addition to having taken strict continence measures relatively quickly and the fact of learning to manage external economic and health shocks, taking measures to protect families, all of the aforementioned is what which makes it clear that many Latin American countries may take less time to recover if compared to what is expected in European countries and the US, however there is a lot of uncertainty, as far as the issue is concerned, however Many of the Latin American countries began to go through the stages of deconfinement for the productive sectors more quickly and with the biosecurity measures that the case warrants, so it is necessary that in the face of the toughest times in recent years, that probably in the face of the greatest health and economic crisis we can remain calm, we can breathe deeply and value the most important things in life, we can control our emotions and be oxygen in our lives and in the lives of everyone around us.

CHAPTER 2

DEALING WITH MY DEMONS

Healing wounds

Emotional wounds generate intense pain that ends up crystallizing inside us. The internal crystallization of our emotions conditions our way of perceiving reality, our behavior, and our decisions.

Among the most common causes that generate emotional wounds are: humiliation, rejection, abandonment, exclusion, betrayal, blame, indifference, comparison and misunderstanding.

When we have these emotional wounds, whether we are children or adults, what we do is generate adaptation and survival mechanisms. For this, two types of responses are generated:

Implosive Response: response of some people consists of submission, self-punishment, and self-rejection; they live in a continuous complaint and are easily resigned.

Explosive Response: response of some people that consists of the emotional impact against other people; the type of response is anger and/or rage, rebellion, confrontations and provocations.

There is a very common way in which we try to counteract our internal pain resulting from emotional wounds, and it is victimhood.

Carlos... It can be said that I was the object of many injuries when I was just a child; I was subjected to verbal abuse by my parents; they always labeled me with words like a liar! disorderly! Disorganized! It's just that you don't have style at all! You're good for nothing! I don't know why they really told me at what point and what could I do wrong when I was only 5, 6 or 7 years old for them to tell me that way... when I got older, things got worse because it was not enough for them to insult me literally, but they also compared me with other children and relatives: Why aren't you as tidy as your cousin? But these are the words that remain in the memory, conscious and unconscious...

When I started to like watching cooking shows as a teenager, and I felt so happy; I saw recipes and researched ingredients, I decided I wanted to be a chef, and then another bombardment began; my mom said: cooks have no future here! With how clueless you are, you will quickly lose your job from burning so much food! And don't mention my dad; that job belongs to women!

I don't remember a compliment, maybe the bad labels erased the good ones, or maybe they never really said anything good to me; this is confusing in my mind... What if I'm sure I never received a hug or an I love you, I never felt loved nor accepted, and that caused such a wound in me that I was not able to love or accept myself for a long time. I had what's called an implosive response.

Used by children and adults; As in Carlos' story, it is a conscious or unconscious personal tendency to hold another person responsible for: how bad they feel, for their unsatisfied needs, for their frustrations; leaving responsibility outside of ourselves, we are victimized.

Victimization is relatively normal in the behavior of children due to the fact that they are children; they have not become completely independent, and they are not independent and reaffirmed adults.

When we are children and we victimize ourselves, we require that they treat us with love instead of judging us. If, when I was a child, something emotionally affected me, and I did not know how to handle the pain by reacting with anger and my loved ones, instead of accepting my pain, react judging my behavior, the wound grew bigger and bigger, so it is not surprising. Continue with more anger.

To educate, first, you have to connect, we cannot stay only in behavior, but we must find a way to understand so as not to cause emotional wounds. Where there was pain, we treated him with love, and when a child learns this, he treats himself well when he is an adult.

Victimization makes no sense when we are adults; there are adults capable of victimizing themselves because of the behavior of their children. When someone becomes a victim, they blame the other person for their feelings; this is the worst form of domestic violence; with violence, children get violent or submissive. When parents victimize themselves in front of their children, they are actually blaming them for making her or him feel bad.

It's amazing how we like to excuse ourselves from everything bad that happens to us or what we do, and we fill our mouths saying: That's how they raised me! I took a lot of punches as a kid! My dad beat me, so I did the same!

Many times it can be said that you have real reasons, perhaps you have been abused, you have been the victim of emotional or physical violence, you have suffered a chronic and/or painful illness, you have not had a comprehensive family, or they took advantage of you. But if you want to live fully, the last thing you can do is blame the past for your failures or bad attitudes.

It's time to let the past go and let healing come into your life! You won't gain anything by feeling sorry for yourself. It's time to leave behind your victim mentality

No one has said that life would be easy; in fact, the same "God said to take up your cross and follow me." Don't compare yourself to another person, and don't think about what could have been. Please take what you have and make the most of it. It may be that you have suffered a lot, that you have many wounds, but do not allow the past to influence your future;

you cannot do anything for what happened but for what will happen.

Let go of the wounds, and to let them go, you must forgive the people who hurt you and, above all, forgive yourself; yourself for the mistakes made; Stop thinking that you are the only one going through this situation and that life is unfair to you.

Meditate on your life; it is true that when we go through a traumatic experience, we need care and affection to be able to recover, but many people do not want to recover, to have all the attention.

Stop mentioning it; unless you let go of the old, the new cannot come. You can't be sad 10 years later; if you really want to be healthy, you have to stop looking back and look to the future.

You cannot relive the old wound, everything is still in your thoughts in the subconscious, and if you think about it again, you feel the same emotion as you experienced it on that occasion. You will be able to feel anguish, hatred, and sadness; you will relive every feeling as if it were that very moment. Therefore, you must let it go!

María... As an adult, I didn't feel fulfilled, I was working in a tourism company, and everything went wrong, or so I thought; my workplace was full of unfiled papers, many times I couldn't find a pen, when They gave me an extra bonus for each order, obviously I didn't earn it, and when my classmates asked me, I simply told them: I've always been disorganized! Since I was little, my mother told me that, and she was right... I had such low self-esteem that I was already affecting my work, social and spiritual life.

I listened to my mother as if she were standing there in front of me telling me: liar! messy! Disorganized! It's just that you don't have style at all! You're good for nothing!

I wanted to start a company, but problems came; I made the decision that I was not going to repeat that; instead of reminding myself of those bad moments, I immediately changed my thoughts to happy moments that I lived at those same ages, moments in which I bathed in the rain with my neighbors, when the teacher kissed me for doing a job well, my elementary school graduation, and there I began to feel new sensations, I changed the negative feelings for the positive feelings that those memories made me feel. I had to consciously make the decision that my mind would go back to painful moments.

This is very important: you must make the decision consciously; if the decision does not come from you, it is impossible for you to heal those wounds, those painful experiences, since those feelings will slow down your progress.

We have two files in our brain:

positive file

It contains our victories, happy moments, triumphs, all kinds of positive emotions and everything that has made us happy.

negative file

Contains our failures, limiting beliefs, harmful words, wounds, and everything that has hurt us is full of pain.

In our life, we must decide which of these two files we will open; many decide to open and reopen the "toxic or negative file", and relive the pain at every moment. On the contrary, they never open the "positive file," so they never think about the good things that have happened to it; they let this important file in life rust.

If you want to be free, send the negative file to the trash and then click on permanent file deletion.

If you really want to heal from the emotional wounds, you have to:

1. Stop making excuses.

2. Stop feeling self-pity.

3. Stop opening the negative file.

4. Stop blaming people and circumstances.

Instead, you must:

1. Forgive everyone who did you wrong.

2. Forgive yourself.

3. Start over, always.

Many times life wants to get us out of that abyss where we find ourselves, and we take the step, but we doubt, and again we fall into distrust; we are so rooted and clinging to the past that we cannot heal ourselves, we live like children still lacking affection and reminding ourselves of what happened to us 10, 20, 30, 40 and even 50 years ago. We remind ourselves of that hug we never received, of those hurtful words of those limiting beliefs.

And there is something that you have to be clear about if you are looking back; you cannot look forward, and you do not realize the blessings that you have today, of that life that you have left to live, and that must be full.

Steps

1-Recognize the negative emotion, and the wounds you have

You must accept that you have a problem that comes from your injuries. If you run away from the problem, you will never be able to deal with it, so face what you feel.

You can't hold back your emotions because then, like a dam that breaks, the water will wreak havoc, so live your mourning, cry, scream and say what you have to say. If, from the beginning, you listen to your emotions, they are already there; they will not need to hurt you; on the contrary, they will weaken.

2-Check if the injury is current or past

If it is something current, you must do something immediately to eliminate and solve that problem; that is, you must set limits and not let the wound continue to advance.

If the case of a mother who bombarded her with bad labels and hurtful phrases and a father who drove away from his dreams with false beliefs was happening right now, I would have very decidedly told them: Stop! That is not so!... At that moment, he is a child who cannot defend himself. Also, as a child, he believes in his parents; who doesn't? But as an adult, he would not have let those words cause wounds and take root inside him.

If the wound is from childhood, we must also set limits, not allow anyone to continue hurting us or hurt ourselves by remembering them as true; for example, if your boss continues to treat you the same as your parents, your partner or your own children, or perhaps you If you keep saying these things to yourself, you must say: Up to here! No more!

The wounds of the past are healed with actions in the present!!

3-Make your wounds a lesson

Ask yourself, why did I live that? Everything teaches us, and this is not the exception to the rule. Many times, what we live through will help us with something; it has made us stronger.

The strongest soldiers pass the most difficult tests, and I am sure that everything has a reason. Maybe when you heal, you will be able to help many people.

You are the one who decides what to do with your experience, or you cling to pain or take it as a learning to be better.

4. Understand the people who hurt us

Sometimes we have to be empathetic and think about why these people acted or are acting in a certain way; this does not mean that we justify it, but it does mean that behind an aggressor, there may be a being who is being or was attacked. If we don't understand this, we may end up being the same; simply because we don't see the reasons, we end up repeating them. Now if we try to understand why they hurt us many times, even accidentally, it becomes easier for us to forgive them and turn the page.

Juan...When I became an adult and tried to save my life, one of the things I understood was that I had to forgive, but how could I forgive something like that? My parents really took my life, curtailed my abilities and made me feel unloved. I inquired why they had done it and discovered something really chilling: My father lived in a country where discrimination was so great that any man could not do "work considered for women" and vice versa, to such an extent that he could be punished, he wanted to be a designer and seamstress and did not know it suffered and did not want me to suffer. And my mother had 12 siblings; she lived alone, like in a battalion, with a lot of people, but in the end alone, she always lost her things in the commotion; her mother forgot who she had hugged and obviously never touched her, a sign of affection. In other words, I didn't know any other way of parenting. That's the only way I managed to forgive them; I know now that they didn't do it badly; I also forgave myself for not having understood it before and living through so many years of resentment.

CHAPTER 3

A LITTLE INSPIRATION

... When I forgive and forgive myself, I started my own path to success; I just need a little inspiration to start my life and the path to happiness.

Many times we wonder what we do in this life, what our mission is, and why we exist. I am going to give you the answer, which was not easy for me to find: Our mission is to have an extraordinary and full life, and we are here to be happy, and knowing what our goals and purposes are is essential for this. This can only be achieved by healing our inner world; when we achieve this healing, all the best in ourselves comes out, and we are capable of being happy and giving happiness to others.

You have to be clear that no one is going to tell you what your dream is or is going to instruct you about the purpose of your life, it must be yourself that you find the answer within yourself, and that answer is achieved from self-knowledge.

When we know our purpose in life, we almost always realize that it has to do with service and that whatever it is, it is always good to help, to make this world a better place every day, and to inspire others to be better. …

…I wanted to fulfill my dreams and help other people, and when I realized that both things could go hand in hand and that they were not independent of each other, I was happy, so I ran after my dreams…

If you feel that you still do not know the purpose of your life, it is time for you to look for it so that you can really feel like a full and fulfilled person. There are books that talk about this, psychologists, videos, etc., but the truth is that you can achieve this if you reach the best of your internal world, and this, of course, translates to the external world. It is important that you understand that even if you have a guide, this is an individual job, that it is you who must get ahead, it is you who must search within yourself, to discover all the good that is in you and deep down to find that purpose.

All this that I am talking about is not easy to find; you must be one within yourself, look for the answer and discover yourself; it requires a lot of dedication and perseverance, of falls and the strength to get back on your feet... You must love yourself and appreciate yourself, but above all, forgive yourself, it is a long process, and along the way, you must enjoy that encounter with yourself because, ultimately, you are the most important person to you.

Self-knowledge of ourselves, we achieve it by being aware of ourselves; this implies thinking about our actions. What actions do I do during the day? How do I feel at the end of the day? Am I really at peace when I go to bed? Our ideals are very important; they give you an idea of what you want and where you are going; you should ask yourself questions like: What do I believe? Do I work for my beliefs?...

This subject must be studied in depth because it is the ideals that inspire our life; without ideals, one cannot live, and these are nothing more than a principle or values that can be achieved and that we move based on. Practically our fuel; without ideals, there is no motivation that moves us. We must also think about our potentialities; potentialities are understood as the capacities that we have as a person, and based on them, we know what we can or cannot do; it is a virtue, a strength, and it is worth knowing your own potentialities and thus making decisions that lead us to perform better in some areas.

And lastly, closely linked to ideals since Motivation is derived from there; What really motivates you in life? What drives you to move forward every day? Do you move in terms of your own motivations, or, on the contrary, do you act depending on what others expect of you? Do you work for your personal development or commitment to others? These are questions you should ask yourself, and it is an essential part of achieving your own self-knowledge.

When you discover that the key is service from your motivation, you will be happy. But what is serving? You are serving:

- When you pick up the dishes.
- When you fix the room, or at least don't mess it up.

□ When you say, thank you, even if you are paying.

□ When you give a smile.

□ When you listen carefully to other people.

□ When you help your friend or friend in trouble.

□ When you call your parents.

□ When you don't throw garbage on the street.

□ When you are attentive to the needs of the people around you.

Service is our mission, and it can be done from the simplest and simplest action to a great impact project; this must be a great purpose, be an inspiration and light for others, and if we can do what we like in our work, It would be ideal, because work would be something we are passionate about.

..You just need a little inspiration.

CHAPTER 4

HOW MUCH DO YOUR DREAMS COST?

We have to set a fixed price for what we want to achieve in life, and based on that, we just create a plan to achieve it.

Just like a game of levels where you start with the easiest level and last the most difficult, that's life; we always have the opportunity to overcome and level up until we achieve our dreams. Many times we feel stagnant, and that we do not advance in level, we feel that we are in a routine, that we are having the same results over and over again: deficiencies, illnesses, heartbreak, negative feelings such as: resentment, hopelessness, discouragement. That's when we have to say stop!

And analyze if we are following our dreams or on the contrary, we are repeating mistakes that do not allow us to level up or advance.

Greece... I was born in full scarcity; for my family, nothing was enough, sometimes not even for half a meal, so the mental pattern was designed for scarcity; I was so rooted and stagnant in this state that even if I got a good job or earned my lottery, the money was not going to yield me and therefore I was prone to lose money easily. All this added to the limiting beliefs that we already talked about and did not let me grow.

It seems incredible, but it is very true that the scarcity mentality attracts scarcity, and the wealth mentality attracts wealth, just as if you love yourself, you attract love from the people around you. Here the problem is not money or love but the mentality we have about them.

So we ask ourselves, how much do our dreams cost? Our dreams cost what it costs to change the mentality; we must change those beliefs and paradigms that have limited us for years and form new beliefs that generate the changes we want; if we see that there are beliefs that limit us, we must be able to recognize and eradicate them in one once for all

This transformation process is a very beautiful and inspiring path if we see it from the point of view that it is for your change. This is where you have to invest and ask yourself again: how much do my dreams cost?

And those dreams will only be achieved from inner healing, self-knowledge and acceptance. Therefore, you should mainly invest perseverance and time to:

- Reading books that inspire you

-Meditation.

-Reflection on your life and self-awareness.

-Do things for you, learn to love you.

Investing this time implies stopping doing other things that you used to do, such as many hours of TV, parties, excessive work (overtime), wasting hours on the networks, and meetings with friends... It's not that these things are bad, but that you must be a disciplined person in this initial process and not do anything that takes away your time for your personal growth.

If you spend time on external things, you take time away from internal things, which is what you definitely want and need to improve.

Focus, discipline yourself and dedicate time to grow; only then can you be able to enjoy the outdoors truly. I assure you that every time you make the right decision in favor of your growth and change a party for an enriching reading or meditation, you will gain confidence in yourself, you will gain energy, love for what you do and true enthusiasm to achieve your dreams.

...I started this process a long time ago, I still have goals to achieve, but I enjoy the journey every day, and I feel proud of each step I take; I have had ups and downs, and many times memories come to my head and limiting phrases like: What nonsense are you doing! This is useless! But you know what is the best of all? Now I am able to recognize when those saboteurs come to mind, or rather I am the object of my own internal sabotage, and I immediately change my

mentality and return to the right path; how beautiful it is to love and accept oneself, only then is one capable of loving and accept the rest of the people!

After knowing and accepting you, you are ready. When you already know your potential, you will be able to shine it and put it to work, equally when you know your limitations, you will be able to transform it for the better and do as they say "of those lemons lemonade," you must know why you are good, what is difficult for you, but above all what are your ideals and that is where your other investment begins…

…I discovered that one of my dreams, and for which I was very good, was to cook and delight others with my food, to serve! Give a little joy to people by savoring delicious dishes made from my own inspiration. That's how I became an entrepreneur; obviously, nothing was rosy; it's not that I said: I was going to undertake, and that's it! In this process, setbacks, difficult decisions, debts, analysis, erasing and rewriting occurred... So when I saw the image of what I wanted to achieve in my mind and on the paper where I had drawn it, I said to myself: This is impossible, no! I can do this out of nothing! And if no one buys! And if they don't like it!

If you allow these ideas of failure and scarcity to occupy your mind, you will stop, and the years will pass, and you will never make a final decision to start; you will always say, "tomorrow I start," and that tomorrow will never come.

Jessica... I found out that if I didn't start, I would never finish and that I also wouldn't have the opportunity to know if this would have been the best, I wouldn't fail, but I wouldn't succeed either, so I started the foundations of my big dream, and those The bases were nothing more than my own faith in myself... In this way, I bought my first utensils, pots, pans, paddles, spoons, mixers and everything that is needed for cooking. I came to think that I was crazy. Well, who buys this first without buying the equipment (kitchen, oven) and having the site? But for me, it was necessary to see something materialize, and that was my way of seeing it and feeling the desire to continue moving forward.

In engineering, you should know that the higher a building is, the deeper the bases or foundations must be. That's life; the higher your dreams are, and the further you want to go, the more you must dig inside yourself and the more internal fibers to mobilize.

Life is a constant construction, and it is the greatest work you will do while you live, so invest in quality materials, dig deep in giving yourself the best of the best and invest the best in yourself: Time and perseverance.

Are you enjoying reading this book?

If you are finding any benefit in it, I would love to receive your support.

I hope you can take a moment to leave a review, if possible.

Thank you for taking the time!

Your review really makes a big difference to me.

CHAPTER 5

MY WINNING PLAN

The first thing that must be done to make a development plan for your life is to know and frame it in BALANCE; a balanced life is very important to achieve happiness. What I mean by this word is that that we cannot tip the scales to only one aspect of our life: It is not only family, not only work, money, fun, or friends... Our life is The union of all this, is made up of all these aspects, and we cannot tip the scales to just one side since we would run the risk of losing our stability; not only do we live on money, not everything is fun or family, our life it is a harmonious balance of all of this, and you must grow as a person in all aspects of life.

The first thing to do is be clear about where you are going, a plan without goals is useless because there is no path to follow, and you would get anywhere. Therefore, from self-knowledge, you must first know what motivates you and what you want to achieve.

After you are clear about this and you must start writing your winning plan:

1. Prosperity: You must think about finances, about having the money to live that prosperous life that you want. Many times we see this as a bad thing. Perhaps many are thinking, if this is a personal development book, why do they talk to me about money as the first step? This resistance is due to the fact that the concept of money and prosperity has been demonized, the misuse of money and the obsession with money that can take us away from what really matters, that is, putting money above everything.

But you really came into this world to be prosperous and happy, not to live in scarcity and calamities. So it is important that in your plan, you establish ways to obtain in a healthy way, what you need to live, a job or business that allows you to live with dignity.

2. Entertainments: You must take into consideration those things that you like and that make you happy, and you will place them within your plan, leaving a space of time for them; perhaps you like to read, go to the beach, write, eat ice cream or a good coffee with your friends, painting, making sculptures are so many things that we like and are passionate about and that we don't dedicate time to. A space of time is essential to do these things. Remember the healthy balance.

3. Social relationships: Cultivating friendships is very important to be happy; we did not come into the world to be alone, we are social beings and need each other. Having friends fills the soul with beautiful things, so don't stop cultivating friendships. Many times because of work, we even forget to call them and meet with those friends, and little by little, they are lost. One I know of the greatest successes in life is developing a good family, loving relationships and good friendships.

Likewise, you need to have good relationships and good communication to undertake, do good business, to reach agreements that will help you in your working life.

4. Maintain good health: You must always have a healthy body and mind; the body is our tool to move through the world, with which we have strength and energy.

We must ensure our care by having healthy habits:

- Good nutrition.

- Abandonment of alcohol, cigarettes and other vices.

It is our obligation to take care of our bodies, drink plenty of water, eat fruit, walk, exercise, and keep our minds active.

One way to stay healthy is to maintain a positive attitude towards life, be positive and optimistic, and love ourselves as we are; this reduces illnesses and is even a great help in patients with chronic and/or terminal illnesses, it has been shown that a good attitude decreases the disease risk and people with cancer have overcome it thanks to this.

You already know how to run, drink water, eat healthily, and to forget the vices combined with positivism will mark the triumph of your plan.

5. Acceptance: This refers to the acceptance that we should have of ourselves and the esteem that we have for ourselves; if we do not manage to love ourselves as we are, nobody will, and we will not have the ability to love the people who are around us. That is why it is important, and I have already mentioned it, that we get to know each other and then come to accept each other. Work on this, and you will see how the rest comes in addition. Love yourself with your strengths and weaknesses and work to eliminate what bothers you, but above all: Love yourself! You are important, a unique being who deserves happiness.

6. Your purpose: A winning plan must result in providing you with a life whose objective transcends yourself and that contributes something to the world; for example, if your plan consists of forming a company and making a lot of money, we might think "What am I going to contribute to the world, what can I do to improve or contribute to the community where I live››, in other words, what values are you contributing with your company?

...When I started my venture in the kitchen and thought about creating a restaurant, my thoughts went back and forth on the idea of being able to make many people happy with my food. I was thinking about -Working on weekends in a family atmosphere where the family could share and find dishes for the smallest of the house. –Working on weekdays with cheap dishes and payment plans for workers who went to eat in their free time. –And carry out social work with a certain number of people with very limited resources in

my community. I was happy to be able to do something for people, and that gave strength and motivation to my plan.

Think about the objective that is above you; what do you plan to achieve or are you achieving.

When you have a purpose and a mission in this world, success comes by itself because the motivation will always be there.

-You must always set a time, or rather, deadlines, to be able to fulfill that plan. Otherwise, you will run the risk of time and even life running out without having reached your goals.

That time must be divided into the short, medium and long term. How long does each time last? It depends on you!

...When I decided to start a business, the first thing I did was to establish my goal completion times. I said to myself ‹‹I am going to write down everything to evaluate my progress››, and that is how I decided that in the Short term (2-3 months): I would buy the necessary utensils and equipment, I would process credit in the bank, and I would look for rented premises. Medium-term (3-12 months): Equip the premises, condition, find 2 assistants, and open the premises. Long Term (1 year and a half): Stabilize profitability, balance inputs and outputs, and start the project to help the needy in the community. (Start with 3 families until increasing monthly). All this allowed me to aim at the target until I did!

When you set goals in terms of meeting the final goal, you can determine what is missing, where you are failing, and what you have achieved, and it gives you the opportunity to make adjustments to the plan.

All this depends on what you consider success; it is not the same for all people, and this is a subjective concept.

...For me, success was getting people to come to my restaurant, creating a reputation for myself in this area, and always having full tables, coupled with being able to feel that I was contributing something to the community where I always lived.

We are talking here about a personal development plan that means growing as a person, evolving, and improving yourself; therefore, it is not something that is obtained overnight; on the contrary, it is a hard path but a beautiful one where you will be able to see growth in every aspect of your life because as I said at the beginning, the plan must seek balance in your life. Every little step you take matters; it's like climbing a mountain, and every little detail matters.

CHAPTER 6

I'M KING OF THE WORLD

Who am I? The answer could be: I am what I do! that is, an artist, a parent, a student, a doctor, a shoemaker... I am what I have achieved! I am a good student, a devoted father, an excellent artist, and a gold-medal athlete... I am my virtues or my defects! An angel or a devil, or maybe I am what other people think of me.

-If we are what others think of us: We will always live to please everyone.

-If our triumphs define us: we would live obsessed only to achieve goals and goals without being happy.

-If our weaknesses define us: we would live depressed since we obviously have weaknesses; we are human, right?

Could we say that we are all these things? How we define ourselves determines the way we face life. You are simply a person, unique and unrepeatable; you were created unique, and there is no one like you; you have your own dreams, your strengths, your weaknesses, your way of laughing, and of crying. You have unique feelings that define you as a person.

And the best of all this is that you are important to the world; you are a fundamental part of the planet; if you did not exist, the Earth would be less complete; it would lack that little ray of light that you give it.

So if you are unique, you should always aim to achieve your dreams because you deserve it...

And the first thing you should do is know your motivation, what motivates you, and what you want to achieve, draw up your plan and achieve it!

Simply because, and when you accept yourself as such and love yourself as you deserve it, you will be able to love others and be in harmony with nature and the whole world; only by loving yourself will you be able to love others and feel like what you are:

The king of the world!

...Who more than me, it seems incredible, now I considered myself important, I knew that I was part of a solution, that I was contributing something to the world, my inspiration was at a thousand, I felt useful and not just another particle in the universe, I knew that I could lift my hands to heaven and not feel ashamed I had forgotten everything I thought I was and was a new person, I let myself be molded in the hands of the potter... And now I was the king of the world.

CHAPTER 7
I WON THE LOTTERY

Life is full of dreams; since we can remember, we dream of different things and events, which of course, we do not have. When we are just children, a common dream is to be able to fly, an ice cream appears out of nowhere, or make your favorite stuffed animal come to life; When we are teenagers, a common dream is, for example, to magically appear somewhere else, perhaps at that party where we weren't allowed to go, to make it look like your favorite actor or platonic love in your house... In short, we dream of being able to meet our basic needs. Obviously, when we reach adulthood, our basic needs are transformed and with them, our dreams... We dream of being millionaires; who doesn't want to be a millionaire? "With money, we can fulfill all our dreams," right?... and it is that it is very common for one to be asked what one would you ask for if one could have three wishes? And our answer is always the same: I would only spend one, I would ask for unlimited money, and with it, I could buy everything I need to fulfill the rest of my wishes!

-Travels all over the world, cruises, good restaurants, a closet full of clothes, eating everything we please, attending concerts, swimming pools, luxurious houses, vehicles... and stop counting. All this without worrying about the bills, and who doesn't dream of that?

...I have not won the lottery, and I am not going to because I simply do not play those things; I believe in my own investment, but I am going to tell you a story...

I am going to tell you the story of Miguel, a young man who became a millionaire and overnight saw his dreams come true, for which he managed to be "happy"...

"Miguel was 23 years old, with a life full of dreams and a marriage on the horizon; he lived at that time with his parents –Martha and Santiago–, and his younger siblings, –Michael and Sofia–; he was already studying the last semester of his accounting career... But his dreams went. Further, he dreamed of the wedding of his dreams, of going on a trip with his family and girlfriend and being able to enjoy everything without money limitations. He dreamed of being on a sunny beach with them, buying different souvenirs, playing volleyball with her little brother and girlfriend, and pleasing her with a bouquet of flowers and a sunset serenade. He dreamed this because he had never been able to have a gesture of this type with her, and even less with her parents and siblings; in addition, although a soon marriage was already in his plans, for him, it was still a dream that was not so close to being fulfilled... <‹How could I marry Angeles, if I don't have a penny, how could I give her a house and equip it? as she deserves if I can't even pay for the honeymoon>>, thought Miguel <<I've never been able to have a gesture of true love with her, a rose or some sweets>>.

That was how Miguel, in search of his longed-for dream and the desire to give the best to his family and girlfriend, began to work the night shift in a fast food store. His life was going between the university and work and he almost didn't even have time to sleep.

One night when he was leaving work, he observed that there were several homeless people looking through the garbage, asking for food and another selling lottery tickets to passing vehicles. Miguel felt compassion, and his reaction was to help a little by buying one of those tickets, which was to win a million-dollar prize. That night when Miguel got home, he daydreamed about what he would do if he won the prize ‹‹ Take my parents on a trip, my brothers and the beach, a romantic dinner and finally, the wedding Angeles will be happy... ››

After that night, Miguel did not see the ticket again; he had kept it in a book and completely forgot about it; he really did not believe in luck, and he was right because luck does not exist; there are only blessings disguised as "luck." Too bad that when we see them as luck and not as blessings, we soon jump into the abyss for being so ungrateful.

Fifteen days later, they were launching the lottery numbers, and they announced a happy and only winner, Miguel for not giving up, and with a certain apathy, I looked for the ticket and checked each number one by one. His eyes were stunned, and his hands trembled to the point that he nearly tore the ticket when he checked for the tenth time that each of his ticket numbers were on the image he had frozen in place. Television.

I won, I won, I won...! were their screams, I can't believe it! That's when the parents and one of the brothers who was in the house came into the room:

"What happened, son? What's up?" -said the worried father thinking that something bad had happened.

-I won the lottery! Michael yelled.

-We won! They all yelled in unison as they hugged each other.

The next day, the first thing Miguel did was call Angeles to tell her; she cried with happiness. Although she did not believe that the money would make the difference between how happy she was going to be in her future marriage, she knew well that it would help them be calmer and far from worries that would divert them from fully living the love they professed for each other and that of the children that they could undoubtedly have sooner than expected.

Fifteen days passed between paperwork, nerves, signatures here and there, the notary, among other procedures... and finally, Miguel had the money in his account.

"Brother, when are we going to the beach?" – Sofia asked – , when you tell me, tell me, tell me…

"Calm down, Sofia; there are many things to do first," Miguel replied dryly.

"But if you already have all the paperwork, remember that it's the last week of vacation; I'll be back to school soon, and then we have to wait until next year; please say yes," she insisted.

– I already told you no, Sofia, if you have to wait, you'll have to wait; there are much more important things now.

That's how time went by, and Miguel didn't show any sign of disbursing any penny; he had in his head the idea that he would do it later and that there was a lot to solve, but the reality is that he didn't want to waste anything or lower the bank account; literally, He didn't buy himself a piece of candy, and every night before going to bed he just looked at his accounts and felt proud of what he had, just looking at her, all of this had become an obsession.

The obsessive inclination to accumulate wealth is really a mania that generates an excessive desire to keep money and other types of wealth such as gold, silver, and precious stones; whoever suffers from it does not spend his obsessive desire to saving and continuing to accumulate, leads him not even to enjoy that money, but rather leads him to a feeling of loneliness, that something is always missing. Family and friendship relationships are greatly affected. In fact, everything that does not contribute to her ideal of saving and accumulating money is underestimated and seen as an offense to her person, and that is how she ends up emotionally attacking her loved ones.

– My love, we have been dating for many years, don't you think we should get married and start a life together if before it was for money, we no longer have that problem. The bride said to Miguel full of dreams. The truth was already many years of swearing eternal love.

– But what kind of proposal are you making? Don't you think we should first think about amassing a fortune? What do you think we're going to live on? Money runs out; it's not eternal.

– My love, don't be like that, with what you earned we could easily buy a house and a car, if you don't want to spend a lot then make it a modest house. You could even fix up your parents' house and give them that vacation they've been waiting for so long.

– You always see things rosy; what is spent without replacing is wasted and does not come back.

– You're right my love, so let's invest part of it in a business, a food sale or something that will make us profit.

– You've gone crazy lately! Do you know how long it would take me to earn money that way, and what if I lose it? You know very well that all investment is a risk, and another thing already makes me tired of that habit of yours of speaking in the plural; it is not let's invest, it will be invested, because I remind you that the money is earned by me.

Faced with these harsh words, Angeles ran away crying inconsolably; she could not believe that her boyfriend since he was almost a teenager, would speak to her this way; they had always spoken in the plural, as a couple, even when someone failed an exam they said: "we failed" and then now this turned out to be a great sin.

Not only Angeles and Sofia had received this kind of response from Miguel, but also his father when he dared to suggest that he buy a car so he could get to university faster, and his mother when she shamefacedly asked him for a new freezer. Since the one they had was getting damaged and the food did not last long.

– Mom, you have had that freezer half working for more than 4 years; why do you want to change it now? You could be thriftier and stay with it until it is completely damaged, then we'll see.

Miguel was not a trace of what he had been. After being an exemplary, loving and attentive son, brother and boyfriend, he had become the complete opposite: a hurtful, stingy, selfish and obsessed person. And it wasn't that he was spending money on it, no! So you see, that would have been less worrisome; the problem was that he didn't spend a single coin for fear of ruining his fortune, and he lived obsessed with seeing his money in his account. His family was worried, and his girlfriend was very hurt and disappointed. Where did those dreams of Miguel end up? Where did those dreams of giving his family a few days of happiness and of finally getting married and creating a nice home with all the comforts?

Miguel was so obsessed with money that he didn't realize the damage he was doing and the moments of happiness he was missing; he didn't know when he stopped dreaming. His brother one day told him:

–Miguel, I think you're having a serious problem with your money. If you continue like this, you'll soon lose Angeles, apart from all the moments we could be living.

-Oh my God! Michael, I don't have a problem; it is perfectly normal to be thrifty; what is not normal is the attitude that all of you have of wanting to spend everything without measure.

–I'm not telling you that; just buy a house, and a car, get married and give your girlfriend a stable and comfortable life and don't keep treating your parents badly.

–I'll do it when I have double what I have now, and that way, the bill won't diminish.

– You realize that if you have a problem, brother, reconsider.

–I already told you that I don't have any problems, and I'm going to have twice as many, I assure you.

Being excessively greedy, never being satisfied, and resentment towards other people for feeling misunderstood are characteristics that are always present in people who suffer from this type of mania. In most cases, people flatly deny having a problem. In fact, they see the problem in others, accusing them of being wasteful, and they think that they are very smart to earn money and save.

Miguel had changed to horrors; his obsession did not let him enjoy life; he got up every morning and went to bed at night thinking about what he had and how to multiply it; his relationship with his family had practically ended, he fought all the time, and with his worse girlfriend, he had already stopped calling her and seeing her. Miguel was no longer interested in his dreams nor in his life; he only lived thinking about accumulating and retaining money that he would not spend. Actually, he was already noticing the difference in the behavior of his family, but as expected, he thought that he was not the one with the problem but that they had changed.

With money, we can live better, and we can have a more comfortable standard of living as long as we control anxiety and obsession with it; otherwise, it can become a real nightmare. If anxiety about money controls us, we will end up losing our lives, our friends, and our family... We will not see money as a tool to live, but on the contrary, we see life as a tool to earn money.

One of those many afternoons in which Miguel walked absorbed in his thoughts, he passed by that street where he bought the winning ticket: <<What if I buy another ticket, that would be a good investment>>, in this way without realizing it began a nightmare from which he would soon want to wake up.

He began to buy a lottery ticket every day, with the hope of becoming a creditor of such a precious prize again, he was very sure that if he had won once, he could do it again, and thus he could fulfill his dreams... He did not realize it that his dream was already there, that he could do all those things that he had always wanted and that he had not done due to lack of money, he already had the money, but his desire to keep it was greater, in this way he lost his family already his girlfriend, withdrew from friends and little by little killed his own dreams. In other words, he loved money more than anything else.

It is the love of money that causes suffering and separation from friends and family; it is not money as such that causes harm since it is a simple tool to supply basic needs. Having a distorted idea about money contributes to the existence of prejudices. The amount of money that someone can have is not really important; what is important here is the attitude that one has towards money and that the person is clear that it is not the money itself that has value but what you can do with it.

If I ask you a question that I heard some time ago in a talk, you might get an idea: Imagine that you are lost in the desert, you are already 2 days old, you are very thirsty, and you have not eaten anything. Suddenly you see in the sand a bale of high-denomination bills and a glass of fresh water, but a note says that you can only take one of the two things. What would you take? The money or the water? I would definitely drink the water since if I am about to die of thirst, what I would do with the money would not be much; it would simply become a simple piece of paper if it cannot be exchanged for things or services, right?

Time passed and Miguel continued to buy lottery tickets secretly and that was how he later ventured into other types of gambling; he began to frequent casinos, and in less than a year, he had already gambled and lost his entire fortune; he had run out of money, without a girlfriend and without the trust of his family who saw what his true self was like with money.

For many people, money is more important than family and life, which is why they live in complete anxiety and imbalance. They are not capable of being happy with the small moments, with what they have; they do not know the full happiness that means sharing ice cream, even if it is small, because it was not enough for more, with the person they love the most.

When he realized that he had lost everything, an immense emptiness remained in his soul, not because of the money, but because now he was completely alone, <‹How different everything would be now if all that money had been spent with my family and my girlfriend››, he reflected, ‹‹by now I would be happily married, but it is too late, I lost her, and I have nothing to start over››. That same afternoon Miguel gathered his family and asked for forgiveness, the parents cried, and behind the brothers, they all hugged each other because they had recovered their son.

"I no longer have anything to give them what they deserve," said Miguel, "I just wanted to have more, but I only lost everything, and I stole the opportunity to be happy. Forgive me!"

– And who told you that happiness is given by money? – said Sophia – , we are happy when we are all together when we have you by our side, when we sit down to eat without any of us missing.

"We love you, son," said the father, "and of course, we forgive you."

Little by little, Miguel is recovering. He had a love of his family back, but his girlfriend was missing, so he went to ask her for forgiveness. With tears in her eyes, she told him these words:

–I will not marry the money, but the man... I will marry you, and we will live together, we will grow together, and if we have money to one-day travel, we will; if not, we will watch the sunset from our window, hugging and looking at our future children grow… That is true happiness… I love you.

Regarding this issue, many specialists in psychology have come to the conclusion that money itself does not bring happiness; it just helps to feel less unhappy by supplying other deficiencies. This means that money alone will never make you feel fulfilled or help you have a fulfilling life.

Many times we ask ourselves, where is true happiness then? And that is where we confuse the concepts of happiness and pleasure. And it is one of humanity's biggest problems, not knowing how to differentiate between these two concepts. We certainly live bombarded with bad influences, such as TV, songs, and the networks, which make us see that we can only achieve happiness with pleasure and make us see bad things as something "normal" that everyone does and for that's ok. Examples: getting drunk (you think of having a lot of money to go from party to party, drinking until you drop), gluttony, lust, etc.

Happiness is really healthy; it is like sweet food, a balm for the soul; it is feeling peace, being calm, feeling that energy that tells you that you are doing well; it is feeling a balance between body, mind and soul. On the other hand, pleasure is a mirage, a delusion; you think you are happy, but that happiness is ephemeral, for example when someone is drinking alcohol, at first, they will feel that they are happy, but when does the bottle run out and the drunkenness that is left over? Happiness would never leave a depressing reaction in the end or give you remorse. On the other hand, the pleasure almost always makes you uneasy and regretful, like Miguel did when he had already spent all his money.

To be happy, it is not only required success, prosperity, or money; happiness comes from the effort to achieve something, from reaching a goal little by little and enjoying the way to it, from the joy of living small moments, from savoring an ice cream, to feel a ray of the sun when you are cold, to live fully and enjoy loved ones.

CHAPTER 8

A BOMB OF EMOTIONS

Joaquin…With all this that I lived through, I found myself in need to seek help and reading; there were things and situations that were not normal for me, one day I was content and happy with the spirit of getting ahead; another day, I just couldn't even get up, I went into depression. I was happy about my venture, but from one second to the next, something told me inside me I won't be able to! This is not sustainable! You are not a little woman! I discovered in my readings that we are simply a bomb of emotions, that we are spiritual and that our mind has great retention, especially of negative emotions.

I share part of what I learned because now in, knowledge is healing.

Emotions are a series of organic reactions, which we perceive as a response to an external incentive; this reaction allows the individual to adapt to a specific situation with respect to another individual, some object or a place.

An emotion is characterized by causing a change in mood for a relatively short time but with greater intensity than a feeling. On the other hand, feelings are the consequences of emotions, which is why they are more lasting and can be expressed.

Emotions are responsible for various organic reactions that can be physiological, psychological or behavioral, meaning that they are reactions that can be innate in each person or can be influenced by previous experiences or knowledge.

Type of Reactions That Emotions Generate

According to psychoanalysis, three types of emotional reactions have been determined:

***Physiological reaction**

It is the first emotional response; it is generated involuntarily; it involves the Autonomic and Endocrine Nervous Systems, generates facial expressions, hormonal changes and changes in the tone of voice.

***Psychological reaction**

It refers to the way information is processed, that is, how what happens at a precise moment is captured consciously or unconsciously according to experiences.

Emotion generates an unforeseen reaction that can be adapted to what surrounds us; they are part of the cognitive processes that the human being performs and that, in addition, is related to the sociocultural context of the individual.

We cannot determine what behavior will cause a specific emotion in an individual, but the emotion expresses the person's state of mind as well as what their current needs are.

Behavioral Reaction

Any emotion that is experienced causes a change of mood and behavior; this is evidenced through body gestures such as: a smile or a narrowing of the eyebrows; people can generally distinguish the facial expressions that accompany the emotions of fear, sadness, joy and anger.

Types of Emotions

It is clear that there are many different emotions; they are classified in a disposition that goes from the basic ones to those properly learned in the different stages and contexts of our lives.

Primary or Basic: These are the emotions of all human beings, that is, those that are congenitally part of their nature and appear in the presence of a stimulus, such as anger, sadness, joy, fear, surprise and aversion.

Secondary Emotions: Secondary emotions are those that follow a primary emotion, such as anxiety that often follows surprise or embarrassment after anger; guilt, pride and jealousy are secondary emotions.

Positive Emotions and Negative Emotions: It is a way of classifying emotions according to the effects they cause on people's behavior; that is, if a person has enough emotional intelligence, they will not let fear control them until they become panic; it is known that fear It is a healthy emotion because it warns us of danger, but if it is not controlled and it turns into panic, then a negative emotion is generated, and it can cause many problems.

‹‹I met a lady who was attacked by a dog as a child; it turns out that in the place where she was born and grew up, people had dogs not with the concept of a family member or pet but rather as guardians to whom almost all of the houses had them chained up during the day and released at night, the dog that bit this lady was kept in chains under the inclement rays of the sun, and with just a little water so that it would not die of dehydration, the point is, that this dog was not treated well and a dog of a powerful breed treated cruelly becomes somewhat dangerous, this lady as a child entered the land where the dog was chained a lot because she lived in a part of it her aunt and she had to bring her any parcels from her father, She was already afraid of the dog because it barked ferociously when it saw her arrive, and one day when she had to take a parcel to her aunt, the dog managed to break the chains that tied him and pounced on her, giving her a bite that took her. After surgery, his recovery was somewhat slow and painful.

When an event of this nature happens to us, we have two options; One is to gradually overcome what happened to us until we are able to heal fully, not only the body but also the mind and heart; for that, we need a lot of emotional help from the people who love us and a lot of knowledge about who we are, that is, to know you, accept you, value you and to love You; The other option to which we have access when such an eventuality occurs is; fleeing to panicland, and submerging each day more in this place, for this it is necessary to deny who we are, reproach ourselves over and over again for what happened, not seeking help, not receiving help or receiving inappropriate help from the people around us.

In the case of the girl I am telling you about, her parents tried to make her lose her fear by confronting him; that is, they forced her to defy the circumstances, going through places where there were guard dogs, among other circumstances that further aggravated her condition. Girl, who grew up believing that all dogs were bad and in her youth suffered a lot since when she went to her friend's houses for any school or university activity, and they had pet dogs, she would panic, completely paralyzing, the story has a happy ending, since in his older adulthood due to things in life he understood that not all dogs are aggressive and that even aggressive ones are not bad, they are only dangerous if their owners mistreat them to the point of unbalance them, Now she works to defend animals, especially dogs, from the mistreatment that some people cause them.

The story would have been completely different from the beginning if this woman had been given emotional support as a child. If her parents were not making such unwise decisions, her fear of dogs would not have ceased to be a normal fear, a fear that causes protection; he would never have migrated to the panic that cost him decades of restlessness.

Emotional intelligence

All animal species, without exception, have intelligence appropriate to the characteristics of their species; this has allowed the species not to become extinct naturally; when I say naturally, I mean that the species that have been in danger of extinction have been the responsibility of We human beings, however, the intelligence possessed by a wolf, which must seek food, shelter, continually migrate to protect from the pack, is not the same as the intelligence possessed by a smaller animal such as a meerkat, which are generally sheltered and one of them will have the important mission of monitoring the environment to warn that a predator or any other danger is approaching.

The human being is not the exception when we talk about intelligence, and very unlike what we once thought regarding the fact that there were people more intelligent than others, each and every one of us possesses abilities, only not all of us are capable of the same thing, and each one learns at his own pace, and a manner which is established by how his intelligence was stimulated in his early years.

Being an intelligent person is being a person aware that we have the ability to learn every day of our lives, to adapt that learning to us, and to be able to adapt to the knowledge acquired; childhood is the learning stage par excellence despite being Humans can learn every day, even until the last day they live, but emotional intelligence is very crucial in our childhood, this is because in our first years of life, we are emotionally dependent. In fact, it is proven that from our mom's womb, we learn basic emotions; this process is through what our mother feels.

Neurolinguistic Programming studies the language of thought, this branch of psychology explains how our unconscious mind is programmed and that these programs are installed throughout our lives, even in our first days of conception when we are in our mother's womb. We learn from her how different emotions feel, which is why we suffer from some conditions that we cannot explain, that we have no idea why we are like this, it is explained by the fact that we have learned with our unconscious mind, For example, emotions, if during our pregnancy mom did not take care of or pay attention to her emotions and she went from being happy to being sad because she felt alone, all this in less than ten minutes,when we are born and we become big we can go from being very happy to being sad in a second or we could be sad whenever we are alone, all this explained by the fact that we learned the emotional state of mom and when to feel it we unconsciously retained this information in our unconscious mind, the unconscious is the part of the mind where all the information to which our conscious mind does not have access is stored, that is, we cannot know what information is retained in that specific area of our mind, but it influences our behavior , attitudes and way of being. All this is explained by the fact that we learned the emotional state of mom and at what moment to feel it unconsciously; we retained this information in our unconscious mind; the unconscious is part of the mind where all the information to which our conscious mind does not have access is stored, that is to say, we cannot know what information is retained in that specific area of our mind, but it influences our behavior, attitudes and way of being. All this is explained by the fact that we learned the emotional state of mom and at what moment to feel it unconsciously; we retained this information in our unconscious mind; the unconscious is part of the mind where all the information to which our conscious mind does not have access is stored, that is to say, we cannot know what information is retained in that specific area of our mind, but it influences our behavior, attitudes and way of being.

When we learn to know ourselves well, that is, when we recognize that circumstances trigger a positive or negative attitude in us. When we can identify the causes, it is easier to deal with negative emotions, so if we recognize that situations such as someone at work getting up from lunch and leaving us alone make us too angry, we can admit to ourselves that this bothers us, then seek an answer to our attitude, for example, perhaps in our childhood everyone ate faster than me and got up from the table leaving me alone, which caused me a feeling of feeling rejected, I could not channel it because I was just a child and my parents or those who could help me not to repress that feeling but rather to heal it,

Destructive Emotions

We say that an emotion is destructive when it negatively affects our relationship with ourselves or with those around us. Every day we have actions without being very aware of them; these actions or thoughts refer to the response of some emotion, for example, saying something offensive to someone who bumps into us, just to cite an example. Now, these actions could be easy to control if we take things easy if we don't let our emotions take control. Many times we end up being victims of our own words, and after we think with a cold mind, we realize that we shouldn't have said a certain phrase or we shouldn't have gotten angry because of that nonsense, but we don't explain why we did it or why. Where did that action come from?

All this that happens with our impulses without almost realizing it usually comes from our unconscious mind; as I explained to you before, our mind is always learning either in a conscious state or with our unconscious part, and in our first years of life, we learn a lot with our unconscious part and today that unconscious mind wants to control you, your emotions will be an instrument with which your unconscious will want to handle you at will, says the author of a very famous book on Neurolinguistic Programming "The Revenge of the Unconscious" that the unconscious wants to have under control everything that happens to us and that we cannot understand.

How then do we get our emotions out of control?

The basic thing to prevent being controlled by our emotions is self-knowledge; this means learning to recognize what life circumstances are when faced with, what episodes make me angry with greater intensity or if some event causes me sadness without knowing how to explain why it is so.

There are thousands of emotional discomforts that we have been dragging on and that are consequences of psychological patterns learned even before birth; they are the cause of everything that affects us in the days of our adulthood;

sometimes, we come across people who are always in a hurry and no matter what time it is, sometimes they are not even aware of the time, but they are very convinced that they are very late. This is explained by many phenomena that his unconscious mind went through at some point, from the fact that his parents wanted him to be born as soon as possible to the possibility that he suffered a lot in his childhood because they labeled him slow and now in the years those who are already an independent individual have to drag through this situation without having the slightest idea why he is like that.

The important thing is not to know why we are a certain way, but to recognize that one suffers from a condition that is not healthy, like always running or becoming sad if left alone, among thousands of anomalies; By recognizing what we have and determining when it happens to us, we will be close to mastering the consequences of our emotions. Only in this way will we avoid collateral damage ranging from being in conflict with ourselves and with the people who love us to arguing with those around us.

When we manage to master negative reactions as responses to an emotion, we will also be able to prevent the people we are in charge of, such as our children, nephews or grandchildren, from taking a negative aspect from us that will also unconsciously drag and control their lives. That is why it is you who must end this terrible evil with which you have to battle.

Mastering My Emotions

We already know that the emotions we feel are not one hundred percent our responsibility; we even know that many reactions we have are not entirely the responsibility of our conscious mind; that is, in certain circumstances, we act under the responsibility of an unconscious or involuntary impulse. , but we also know that we are responsible for what we do with our emotions or rather, we are responsible for what we let our emotions do to us; we must take control of our emotions, or they will take control of our actions, and they will harm us, hurting ourselves and all our loved ones. So take control, you can and you should.

So:

1.) Watch yourself:

Observe the moments in which you lose control; this happens to you: before all the basic emotions. Is it only when you feel anger or fury? Is it only in the face of sadness? Obviously, when an unexpected and negative event happens to us, such as the death of a family member or friend, it should prompt us to cry, either in public or when we are alone, it would be abnormal not to experience this emotion, but it is not normal for an adult to start crying. To sing and in public, if something happens to you like failing an exam in a course or even at the university or crying in panic in the presence of an insect or a domestic animal such as a dog or cat, if this happens to you, you should work more on you must try to find the cause of your imbalance, and if you cannot find it, at least you must recognize that this is not healthy.

2.) Love yourself:

Do not blame yourself for your defect; you know that you are like that for a reason, even if you do not know why, do not blame yourself or mistreat yourself, but do not justify yourself either; you can and should change, and with the appropriate help, you will achieve it.

3.) Master Yourself:

When you know what triggers the negative reaction to your emotion in you think and control yourself; for example, you are angry that someone in the dining room of your work or university or in any place where you have to eat with a group of people, get up from the table without everyone having finished, either because your dad scolded you

If you stopped before he finished, or on the contrary, you were sad because they left you alone, think, those people who are with you today have no idea that they are hurting you by getting up before you finish. They also have problems, you are going to judge them because they have to stop to continue working or to call their children, or they have to run to the bathroom as soon as they eat, or a thousand reasons that, like you, they could not know what is happening to you, unless they You tell him that it bothers you if they stop if they didn't all finish, which is not recommended if you aren't friends in the first place. Now you must convince yourself that they are not leaving you alone on purpose; you must adopt an empathetic attitude and put yourself in their place; only then will you understand them, and the sadness or anger will disappear.

4.) Seek Help:

Finding the situations in which you feel that at some point you have lost control of a certain emotion is apparently something simple, but it is not always like that, and even if it were, it is not always easy to control yourself when you feel that it is escaping from your hands. , that you will not be able to control yourself, seek emotional help from a good psychologist, currently there are many experts in Neurolinguistic Programming, and in emotional help, in addition to professional help, you need help from a friend who listens to you and you even need a family member, in Finally you need to feel understood, loved and accepted, but more importantly you must learn to listen and love yourself.

5.) Live:

Now that you know that you are sufficiently capable of controlling your emotions and the impulses that they cause in some people, it is time for you to relax and start living; the past does not have absolute control of your life, but the present does because determine tomorrow, so focus on living fully today, enjoy the company of your family, take a deep breath in the face of every situation that threatens to rob you of your peace of mind. We were born to be happy, and if you cannot be happy, it is because there is an imbalance in your lifestyle; if it is emotional, you can repair it, and as I already told you, you have a duty to do so.

It is well known that anger leads to a reaction that is somewhat difficult to control, but as with all emotions, if we do not control it, it will control us, and we will have terrible consequences.

Anger is an instinctive response that human beings have and that basically occurs as a protection or defense mechanism against certain threats; it can vary from a brief irritation to a violent act if we allow it to get out of our control, it will cause us: big problems social and also possible disorders in our health.

When we let anger grow to the point of becoming anger, the following abnormalities occur in our bodies:

+ Increases blood pressure (Blood Pressure); this can bring consequences in the short or medium term and, in the long term, causes deterioration of the arteries.

+ Elevated heart rate, which instantly produces tachycardia

+The production of chemical substances such as adrenaline is increased, which means the natural balance of the body is affected.

+ You suffer from contractures, pain in the muscles and disorders such as headaches and migraines.

+ The respiratory system increases, which causes the heart to pump more intensely.

+ The risk of suffering diseases such as gastritis, colitis and dermatitis increases.

+ Take some time before answering: it means to think first and answer later; someone once said: "Never decide something when you are very happy or very angry." If you consider it convenient, leave the place, take a breath, recover your peace of mind and face the situation again with a cold mind.

+ Relax: performing conscious and deep breathing techniques, to relax it is convenient to repeat positive phrases to yourself; this will help you change your attitude towards the problem.

+ Do some sport: Doing some sporting activity releases endorphins

+Use your sense of humor to lower the tension in you: many people believe that whoever jokes about their problems is not a serious person who looks at problems superficially, but in reality, this technique allows one to look naturally at what is happening.

+ Think about what makes you angry: just as you mentioned in the general way of mastering emotions, the aspect of analyzing what circumstances make you angry will help you a lot since it leaves you in a scenario in which you will know what to expect, and that is more easy self-control

+Learn to forgive: we must learn to be tolerant of others, accepting that not everyone thinks and acts the same; the empathy and willingness you have to understand other people will help you to know why.

CHAPTER 9

THE HELM OF MY LIFE

We all want to live to the full, but we do that know that only when we take control of our own lives; we cannot think of living to the full if other people, situations or emotions manage our lives at will. Here I give you some little tips.

1. Set limits: many times, it is difficult to set limits, but more than necessary, you must learn to say "NO" in many situations, many times in the name of friendship, they demand too much of us, and we fill ourselves with commitments that in the end we cannot fulfill, or they make us damage. You must decide which commitments you assume and which ones you don't, to whom you lend money or not.

2. You must design your own life: Create your own life and decide which path to take, life is definitely yours, and you only have one; everyone lives their life, and it's only fair that they let you live yours. So it is you who must go your own way. Take the reins of your destiny.

Carlos... When my parents made fun of my love for cooking when I was a teenager, my father forced me to start a law degree because he wanted a lawyer in the family. You can't imagine how unhappy I was; it wasn't my life, it was like living in their life, and it wasn't fair. It was when I gave a STOP to the situation I took control of my life and began to be what I wanted above the bad omens, which told me that I was not going to make it.

It all starts with your mind and the way you want to see life and visualize yourself.

3. Change all your past wounds into lessons: We have already seen everything that happened to us before; we must transform it into learning; we cannot be the victims all our lives; we must get up and use each failure as a step to climb.

4. Live to the fullest: Live every minute, enjoy every moment of your life, every breath, every sip of water. If you want to scream, scream, if you want to dance, dance, enjoy it's your life, allow yourself to be happy and also cry with a movie, without fear of what they will say... It's your life; live it! Enjoy with your family and with your loved ones. Don't be afraid to say I love you! I need you!

CHAPTER 10 WAKING THE WOLF

Humans, like wolves, are social beings; we need to remain organized in groups and follow guidelines or rules of coexistence in order to live and prosper. With the passing of time, human beings forget much of what God naturally placed in us, such as the well-being that we have when we are with our family or friends; what for wolves is a pack, although some of us seem to have forgotten the fact that we naturally need to live in society internally we know it because somehow even if we are the most apathetic and antisocial being in the earth, we must recognize that alone we cannot do everything we need to survive.

From the wolves, we can re-learn:

How important is communication:

For wolves, howls do not just mean making noise; their howls are a faithful test of their communication skills; although it may seem incredible, each wolf howls differently, and the way they howl is different depending on what they want to communicate.

Maintain a healthy balance between work and play:

Wolves, like the vast majority of animal species, work to earn their food; in their case, their job consists of traveling to find protection and food, they can travel 50 kilometers a day, and along the way, they must fight for the survival of the pack, since they go through great dangers, but this does not prevent them from stopping to play in small spaces, this is an important part for the development of puppies and for healthy coexistence, since through this process, they create strong bonds between them.

The importance of teamwork:

For a wolf, the concept of teamwork will always be clear; they divide responsibilities and understand that the success of their objectives depends on teamwork; it is written in their DNA that working in a pack allows them to obtain better results.

There are few wolves that have defied their packs and have been expelled from it for him, which we call the Lone Wolf, and they are strange in nature; it is practically impossible to hunt, and he ends up making a great physical effort that would eventually cause his life.

Perseverance in what can be changed and acceptance of what cannot be changed:

The life of the pack of wolves is not an easy life; every day, the goal is to survive, and in the hunts, they fail more often than they succeed. In fact, it has been proven that the chances of succeeding in the hunts are less than 14%. Between 3% to

14%, but we will never see a pack of Wolves giving up; we will not see a wolf blaming another for their failure; they simply learn from their mistakes; they do not give up and progress. Wolves are the best teachers when it comes to persevering and learning from their own mistakes and those of their fellow men.

Awaken the wolf in you!

CHAPTER 11
BETTER THAN EVER

While it is true that we cannot have all the circumstances that we experience every day under control, it is also true that once we manage to work our lives emotionally, we can control how we react to what happens to us, our state of mind is primarily responsible for how The day goes by, that is, how we feel emotionally influences our decisions and therefore much of what happens to us and obviously in our relationship with others.

To change a negative emotional state such as sadness (which is not convenient to eliminate, it is only healthy to prevent it from controlling us), it is necessary to discover what causes that emotional state, what is the origin of sadness after you have identified the causes it will be easier for you to find a solution, it will always be necessary to think that only we have control of what we decide to do with our emotions, that only we can determine if we stay crying all day or not, now, it is true, that not only with our thinking we would be able to change our state of mind even if we proposed it intensely but obviously with positive thoughts and a discipline of habits

Structured that we form a new routine plus the appropriate help, we will be able to influence our state of mind if we begin to use focused guidelines and modify our habits by adding new routines to our days, then I will list a series of recommendations that will help you stay in a state positive emotional day.

1) Good Humor: look for activities that relate to good humor, such as spending some time each day watching some comedy on television or reading healthy and funny jokes, talking for a while listening to a friend who always makes you laugh.

2) Accept what makes you sad: sadness has a specific function that is very important; it helps us understand what our needs are and reflects what event made us feel so bad, so knowing what caused us sadness, we can be aware of not allowing it to happen to us again, accept, forgive and let go.

3) Move more: it is not about exercising in the gym, but in simple activities like going for a walk or doing any outdoor recreational activity; it is about not getting stuck in a situation.

4) Focus on positive things: the human brain always seeks to be consistent with our emotional state, so if we are happy, we will see everything around us very positively, but if we are sad, we will only be able to see everything sad in life even if it is an event that has 90% chance of going well, we will focus on the 10% chance that it goes wrong, we must exercise our minds to look for positive things, to remember good things that happened to us and focus our thoughts on that.

5) Living in the present: Sadness and anxiety are two emotional states that go very hand in hand; human beings

tend to live in the future, and we get anguished thinking about everything that could happen. If we find ourselves in a sad emotional state and think about the future, anxiety will rise in us; we must live in the now so as not to give our mind more room to imagine negative and 0.05% possible scenarios.

6) Dedicate time to leisure: leisure activities are as important as any other activity, just try not to always do them alone since the company is good emotional therapy.

There are difficult days in which you will only want to abandon everything, and I do not blame you; you will have justified reasons; life is not easy. In those moments, you may think that there is no future and you have no hope left; you will think that everything is impossible, that every step you take is going nowhere, and that your goals are unattainable. Situations where you feel that everything has turned upside down, that nothing works out for you, and everyone is against you... That is the moment you have to persevere and persevere, that is: if I want to and I can.

To persevere is to have hope; it is to smile at life even though everything is bad, to shout from the four winds that everything will be fine, that you can, that you are capable of being happy in difficult situations and in good situations. In situations of anguish and sadness because you have faith that everything will improve and it will be a learning experience, and in good times because you are capable of being thankful. Persevere, trust yourself, and your ability to grow and achieve what you set out to do.

Leave behind the fear of being happy, the fear of freedom, dare and get out of the dark zone, where they put you in the past and where you keep putting yourself in the present, where it seems that the light will never come out, where you don't grow ...Be yourself, don't be afraid, don't be afraid of criticism, accept yourself as you are, make your decisions and live.

Did you enjoy reading this book?

If you are finding any benefit in it, I would love to receive your support.

I hope you can take a moment to leave a review, if possible.

Thank you for taking the time!

Your review really makes a big difference to me

With love and gratitude…

Made in the USA
Las Vegas, NV
16 January 2024

84450736R00056